▲▲▲

The
Native American
Book of

Change

▼▼▼

NATIVE PEOPLE ▲ NATIVE WAYS ▲ SERIES

VOLUME III
◄————————►

▲▲▲

The Native American Book of

Change

▼▼▼

TEXT BY

White Deer of Autumn

ILLUSTRATIONS BY

Shonto W. Begay

▲ Beyond Words Publishing, Inc. ▲

Published by
Beyond Words Publishing, Inc.
13950 NW Pumpkin Ridge Road
Hillsboro, Oregon 97123
Phone: 503-647-5109
To order: 1-800-284-9673

Page Layout: The TypeSmith
Cover Design: Soga Design

Printed in the United States of America
Distributed by Publishers Group West

Library of Congress Cataloging-in-Publication Data
White Deer of Autumn.
    The native American book of change / author, White Deer
of Autumn ; illustrator, Shonto W. Begay.
        p.   cm. — (Native people, native ways series ; v. 3)
    Summary: This third in a four-volume series on Native
Americans focuses on their attempts over the centuries to retain
their culture in the face of a changing world.
    ISBN 0-941831-73-6 (v. 3) : $4.95
    1. Indians of North America—Religion and mythology—
Juvenile literature.   2. Indians—Religion and mythology—
Juvenile literature.   3. Prophecies—Juvenile literature.
[1. Indians of North America—Ethnic identity.]   I. Begay, Shonto,
ill.   II. Title.   III. Series: White Deer of Autumn. Native people,
native ways series ; v. 3.
E98.R3W47   1992
970.004′97—dc20   92-17001
                                                            CIP
                                                            AC

I gratefully acknowledge my wife and children for their understanding of the changes I go through. For we all realize that change is the one constant.

CONTENTS

PART I

← →

Poets, Prophets, and Peacemakers After the Conquest

▼▼▼

CHAPTER 1

⬅━━━━➡

History and Prophecy

▲▲▲

**If you don't know the past, then you
will not have a future. If you don't know
where your people have been, then you
won't know where your people are going.**

—from *The Education of Little Tree*,
by Forrest Carter

▼▼▼

W hat is a prophecy? It is the predicting or telling of
an event before it happens. Now we will look
carefully at history and at how the prophecies of the
American Indians during and after the conquest of their
lands foreshadowed the ending of an age.

Imagine that you had a dream in which everything
you knew and loved was suddenly taken away. All the
posters and art decorating your school and home were

stripped from the walls by strange-looking men. They went to your places of worship and tore apart the art and the altars, smashed the statues and the crosses! They threw all the books and magazines from your library, even the favorites that you keep in your room, into a big fire and burned them! Then these strangers pulled down your country's flag, tossed it into the fire too, and hoisted up their own flag.

Imagine that in your dream those strangers carried strange weapons which you'd never seen before. Soon you see how they kill, exploding like thunder and ripping into the flesh and hearts of those you love. You see your parents killed and yourself snatched away to become a slave who works only for the wealth of these strangers.

Oh, what a dream!

When you wake you are trembling and crying. Your sheets are wet with your sweat.

Indian prophets had such dreams. Their dreams told them what was going to happen — to the People, to the land, to the culture.

The prophets felt the anguish and grief of the elders in their dreams and the agony and pain of the women and children. Their dreams showed the warriors fighting valiantly to stop the invaders. The prophets felt the desperation of war. They saw their people losing the sacred land.

The prophets could smell in their dreams the stench of death from dying and decaying animals. They could

hear in their dreams, the earsplitting sounds of countless trees crashing to the ground in the forests.

The prophets saw in their dreams the conquerors and colonizers burying the temples and the cities beneath tons of earth. They saw many of their sacred objects destroyed and others stolen away.

They saw the wisdom of the ages rising in black smoke from burning books. As the colorful symbols and pictures turned to gray ashes floating through their dreams, they watched their cultures blow away in a terrible wind.

Poets created poems to stir the emotions of the People. Songs were sung to protect the People. Peacemakers struggled to unify the People.

Awful things happened so fast. Sometimes within days, sometimes within months, the temples were gone. The cities were ruined. Cultures were destroyed.

Why couldn't they stop it? Why couldn't the People prevent their doom?

Maybe it happened too fast. Soon after the arrival of the Europeans in the lands of the Native Americans, the world for the People changed. No, it did more than change; it was turned upside down and inside out.

Our brief journey through history and some of the prophecies that foreshadowed the conquest of Native America will not be a happy one. It will be painful, just as your imaginary dream was painful. But the journey is necessary, for if we don't know where we've come from, we'll certainly not know where we're going.

Come with me now through time and mind,
for the past beckons to be known.
And the future,
crouched like a panther on the bough of a tree,
waits to see if we . . .
if we
have truly
grown
while it growls
impatiently.

CHAPTER 2

← →

The Conquest

▲▲▲

They came out of nowhere
telling us how to eat our food
how to build our homes
how to plant our crops.
Need I say more of what they did?
All is new — the old ways are nothing,
they are changing
be not too hard.

> **— from "Indian Love Letter,"**
> **by Soge Track**

▼▼▼

Instead of the Native names for the Great Mystery, instead of the names of the sacred beings like Quetzalcoatl, Kukulcan, and Deganawida ringing in the land as they had for centuries, the Europeans brought a new religion. The new religion had other names. Many of its followers didn't tolerate the beliefs of the Native Americans. Often they forced the Native people either to abandon their old ways or to die.

In Mexico and in Central and South America, it is estimated that within a hundred years of their arrival in the "New World," the Spanish, following their "divine right of discovery," were directly responsible for the deaths of several million Native Americans. In reality, this "divine right of discovery" enabled the Europeans simply to claim for themselves all the Native American countries they had invaded. They called Indian land their own because they believed that God and their kings gave them this "divine right." The Indians' rights as possessors of the land for uncounted generations were ignored or declared non-existent.

These European invaders felt that they had the "right" to kill Native Americans. They believed that the Native people of America were not human because they were not Christian. They regarded Native Americans as human only if they became Christian. Most of the People who would not accept Christianity were killed or forced into slavery. Often they willed themselves to die. For many, it was better to die than to live as a slave.

In some places the Spanish allowed the missionaries to baptize the Indians, whether or not they wanted to be baptized, before they were "put to the sword."

The Mayan epic *Cuceb* foretold the future. As with most prophecies, it is like looking through a cloud or heavy mist. The poet saw the end of an age coming, but not who or what would cause the end to happen.

> . . . comes the wind, the rain, comes the
> telling of destinies. . . . Then there will be a
> new reign, a new teaching, according to the
> word of the priest Chilam Balam. . . .
>
> When it comes, the walls will be destroyed
> and the house thrown down, when destruc-
> tion comes over the lords of the land. . . .

What was it like for the American Indian to see into the future? It's impossible to imagine how the prophets must have felt upon seeing that glimpse of what was to be. Even the people who listened and who read the poems and who saw the signs themselves probably did not fully understand how the end would come or just how horrible it would be.

In the Aztec poem "A Song for Huetzotzinco," the poet explained the devastation and loss that was to come. Remember that the Europeans had not yet arrived, and the poet, no doubt through a dream or vision, wakes seeing something in the future, like catching a glimpse of what has yet to happen. It evoked in him such a prophecy:

> And you Aztecs, may you remember con-
> cerning us when you descend and suffer be-
> fore the majesty of The Giver of Life, when
> you shall howl like wolves.
>
> There, there will be only weeping as your
> greeting when you come, there you will be
> accursed, all of you, workers in filth, slaves,
> once rulers of warriors, and thus our beauti-
> ful city will be deserted.

O friends, do not weep, but know that
sometime we shall have left behind us the
things of our nation, then the waters shall be
made bitter and the food shall be made bitter,
as never before, by The Giver
  of Life.
  . . . in a little while our people shall be seen
in the fire, amid the howling of wolves.

Another poet who foresaw the destruction of Native America was a Mayan priest named Nam Pech. His prophecy has to do with the ancient Mayan city of Chichen Itza, located in the Yucatán Peninsula.

Ye men of Itza, heed the tidings,
Listen to the forecast of this cycle's end;
Four have been the ages of the world's
  progressing,
Now the fourth is ending, and its end is
  near. . . .

Of course, like any brave people, the Native Americans who first greeted the Europeans on these shores as brothers weren't about to allow this conquest to happen without defending themselves. Many quickly saw Cortés and the Spanish, not as the return of Quetzalcoatl at all, but as conquerors and thieves who would go to any extreme to acquire gold and any other precious metal handcrafted by the Indian artists.

Few people know how much the Indian gold and silver changed the course of world history, especially in

Europe. According to the book *Indian Givers*, by Jack Weatherford, shortly after the colonizers landed here, the gold treasure in Europe increased by 200 million tons — that's tons! Aztec silver alone was made into coins worth at least two billion dollars!

What the Europeans didn't realize, perhaps because they were so blinded by greed, is how differently the two worlds viewed these metals. Indians wore gold or sculpted it into wonderful pieces of art. It was not an expression of wealth. Native Americans believed gold to be the excrement, or waste, of the mighty Sun. Some Natives referred to gold as the "sweat of the Sun." Wearing it or sculpting it was a sign of the Indian's humility and a creative returning to the gods who created earthly beauty.

The Indians took only the gold, silver and turquoise that was made available to them by the Earth — sort of like her fingernail clippings. They did not believe that humans should dig deep holes into the body of the earth, such as mining, for example. Such an act would violate her body and would make her sick.

For many Europeans, gold had a very different meaning. It meant wealth. Even today Indians are dying because of this lust for gold and the material wealth it provides. In the jungles and rain forests of South America, entire tribes are vanishing. The land itself is being destroyed—all for gold, for wealth.

Much like the modern-day gold seekers, who care little about how they affect our world, the conquistadores went to any extreme to get the precious yellow metal from the Native Americans. However, instead of destroying the land they plundered the Indian cities. The stolen and artfully created gold and silver pieces were melted into bricks and shipped back to Europe. This caused the greatest economic boom in history! It also created a boom in the slave market, which not only doomed the Indians, but devastated the lives of many Africans.

Naturally, Indian conflicts and wars with the invading Europeans were the result. In these violent clashes, far more Indians died than did Europeans who sought to seize their lands. The death and destruction was enormous. The Spanish are responsible for the deaths of millions of the People. They killed with the sword, with their infectious diseases, with their inhuman system of slavery.

At least a million Carib Indians, for example, perished within ten years of the Europeans' arrival on their islands. Today the Caribbean Sea and the Caribbean Islands are named for them. But most of the Native American people are gone. Only a few Caribs still inhabit some of the islands. Some escaped to South America, where they intermarried and live to this day in the blood of other peoples. There are also Carib descendants, it is said, who maintain their culture as a distinct and isolated tribe in the country of Belize.

The conquest of the Western Hemisphere by the Europeans was no different in North America. Here too, Native prophets saw the destruction coming. Like the Aztec poets and Mayan priests, they too had dreams. These are described in Chapter 3.

CHAPTER 3

North American Prophecies

▲▲▲

Brothers, these people from the unknown world will cut down our groves, spoil our hunting and planting grounds, drive us and our children from the graves of our fathers and our council fires, and enslave our women and children.

— from "Prophecy of Metacomet," a Wampanoag warrior-sachem and a son of the Massasoit Osamekun, the Native leader whose kindness and generosity enabled the Pilgrims to survive

▼▼▼

Metacomet's prophecy was fulfilled. A war to try to keep it from happening would bear his English title and name, King Philip. The result of his struggle and those that followed left a bloody trail from one end of the Native American continent to the other.

It began with the newcomers' belief in their "divine right of discovery" and was intensified by their proclaimed doctrine of "Manifest Destiny." With these ideas rooted in their minds, the new colonists and later U.S. citizens—land speculators, pioneers, gold seekers, missionaries, soldiers, and immigrants of all kinds—poured into the lands and country of the Native American.

These new people also brought new and fascinating things. The colorful glass beads, iron utensils and tools, as well as coffee were quickly adopted into Native American life. Even the basic teachings of Christianity, because they profess love and not killing or stealing, appealed to some of the Indians. These ideas were already a part of the Indian way.

Yet, there were many Native Americans like the Seneca orator, Red Jacket, who appreciated the Indian belief in the Great Mystery. He felt that missionaries should work among the white man rather than among his people, for Red Jacket saw his people cheated and robbed. Like many Native Americans, he saw other things that the white man brought besides a new religion. Some were very dangerous and harmful, such as alcohol, guns, and diseases, and strange new ideas about something called "owning" the land.

The conquest of the Western Hemisphere took more than 400 years. Of the estimated 2,000 Native American tribes and nations who thrived here before 1492 when

Columbus landed, 1,700 of them have been wiped off the face of the earth. These tribes are gone forever. Only some of their names remain: Calusa, Illinois, Peoria.

The conquest continues. It continues everywhere the American Indians lose their land. It occurs every time their sovereign, native rights are lost in North, Central, or South America. In Guatemala, El Salvador, Nicaragua, and South America, the rights of Native Americans are too often ignored. In many of these places the People are still being oppressed and killed. Until this century, in Brazil it wasn't even a crime to kill a Native American.

The conquest continues through the loss of Indian culture. The Oglala Sioux chief Luther Standing Bear wrote about this loss in his own kind of prophecy:

> When the Indian has forgotten the music of his forefathers, when the sound of the tomtom is no more, when noisy jazz has drowned the melody of the flute, he will be a dead Indian. When the memory of his heroes are no longer told in story, and he forsakes the beautiful white buckskin for factory shoddy, he will be dead. When from him has been taken all that is his, all that he has visioned in nature, all that has come to him from infinite sources, he then truly will be a dead Indian. His spirit will be gone, and though he walk crowded streets, he will, in truth, be — dead!

Like Luther Standing Bear, the great Suquamish and Duwamish chief Sealth, often called Seattle, believed that the Indian too "has been somewhat to blame" for what has happened. He meant that sometimes Indians, like any people in history, have been their own worst enemy.

Some Indians served as warriors against their own kind. They fought against other tribes. They fought for revenge. Sometimes they fought because they were jealous. Other Indians became valuable scouts for the soldiers, tracking down their own people. Some did this because their families were threatened by the soldiers if they didn't. Some Indians became missionaries and sought to change the old ways. Others carried out the wishes of the government, for they were taught by government schools to be ashamed of their Native heritage. They wanted little to do with their Indian beliefs and culture, and they were paid to make their people feel the same. A few Indians abandoned their culture for money and power.

Thus, the Indians aided in the devastation of other tribes and nations. What Indian in Mexico does not know the name of La Malinche? Also called Dona Marina, she was the mistress of Cortés. Born a Native American and later Christianized, she served as a translator and informer against her Mayan and Aztec people. Without her inside information and knowledge, perhaps Cortés might not have succeeded in his bloody tear through Mexico and the Yucatán. To this day, one of the worst names to call a woman in Mexico is "La Malinche."

Sacajawea, a young Shoshone woman, is credited with having guided the Lewis and Clark expedition across the Rocky Mountains. If it hadn't been for her knowledge of the trails and of the People's languages and ways, the

United States would not have expanded so quickly and the Indian nations of the West would have lived longer.

Keokuk was recognized chief of the Sauk nation by the United States government while the real chief, Black Hawk, was away defending his country. For the power of being a chief recognized by the U.S. government and for his own greed, Keokuk sold almost all the country that belonged to his people!

At age seventeen, Black Hawk had led his first war party against U.S. government soldiers. Like the Wampanoag warrior-sachem King Philip, Black Hawk was so respected by his enemies that a war was named for him. It was called Black Hawk's War, but the war wasn't his to win. As an old, tired Sauk warrior, he gave his surrender speech in 1832. In it he revealed the heart of a true warrior and foretold what was to be:

> He [Black Hawk] feels for his wife, his children, and friends. But he does not care for himself. He cares for his nation and the Indians. They will suffer. . . . He can do no more. . . .

According to *Chronicles of American Indian Protest,* by the Interracial Council on Books for Children, Black Hawk was imprisoned by the U.S. government. He was later freed, but never regained his position of leadership among the Sauk people. In 1838, Black Hawk died in poverty. After his death, Black Hawk's grave was robbed and his remains put on display in an Iowa museum. And Keokuk? A bronze bust of him was made and placed in the Capitol in Washington D.C. and a town in Iowa now bears his name.

Although American Indians were partly at fault for the loss of their country, their initial offer of friendship and trust may have been their greatest mistake. Their often peaceful and friendly acceptance of the "New World" Europeans as their brothers allowed everything else to happen.

Twenty years after Black Hawk's surrender, Big Elk of the Omaha foreshadowed the suffering that was to come:

> I bring to you news which it saddens my heart to think of. There is a coming flood which will soon reach us, and I advise you to prepare for it. Soon the animals which Wakonda [the Great Mystery] has given us for sustenance will disappear beneath this flood to be no more, and it will be very hard for you. . . . I tell you this that you may be prepared for the coming change. . . .

Chief Sealth not only recognized how Indians were partly at fault for their destruction and for the dangers that were to come, but he also prophesied the possible end of the red race. This idea of the extinction of the Indian people is unimaginable for some. But remember that by the twentieth century the extinction of the North American Indian was near. In his famous oration "The White Man Will Never Be Alone," Chief Sealth expresses this prophecy:

> And when the last Red Man shall have perished, and the memory of my tribe shall have become a myth among the White Man, these shores will swarm with the invisible

> dead of my tribe. . . . At night when the streets
> of your cities and villages are silent and you
> think them deserted, they will throng with the
> returning host that once filled them and still
> love this beautiful land.

While Chief Sealth may have envisioned the end of the Native Americans, with only their ghosts remaining, he observed the end of the white man's civilization as well.

> Why should I mourn at the untimely fate
> of my people! Tribe follows tribe, and nation
> follows nation, like the waves of the sea. It is
> the order of nature, and regret is useless. Your
> time of decay may be distant, but it too will
> surely come. . . .

Regret is indeed useless now. We cannot change what has already been. But we can all learn from history and go on, always trying to understand, always learning from the past.

What went through the minds of the Mayan priests Chilam Balam and Pech when they awoke from their dreams? What did they think when they saw the future, when they saw the destruction of all they had known, when they saw the ruins of their great city Chichen Itza? How hard did the Aztec poets struggle to find the words to describe their dreams? How did the words come "amid the howling of wolves"? What were the feelings of Metacomet, Black Hawk, Big Elk, and Chief Sealth when they saw that the end of their world was near?

We can only imagine.

CHAPTER 4

More Warnings and Prophecies

▲▲▲

Brothers, we are friends; we must assist each other to bear our burdens. The blood of our fathers and brothers has run like water on the ground, to satisfy the avarice of the white man. We, ourselves, are threatened with a great evil; nothing will pacify them but the destruction of all red men.

Brothers, many winters ago, there was no land; the sun did not rise and set: all was darkness. The Great Mystery made all things. The white people were given a home beyond the waters. This land was given to the red children. We were given the strength and courage to defend them.

> **Brothers, my people wish for peace; the red men all wish for peace; but where the white people are, there is no peace for them, except it be in the bosom of our mother.**
>
> —from an oration by the Shawnee leader Tecumtha (which means Panther Lying in Wait)

▼▼▼

American Indian prophets prophesied the destruction of their nations and their lands. Through their dreams and visions and sometimes through their understanding, they knew what was to come. Many times their prophecies became reality. But some spoke of ways to rise above such destruction.

In many places in North America poets and men of vision who saw into the future appeared. They, like the people they tried to help, were true natives of this land. Some of the prophets' names are etched in the minds and hearts of the People, but one remains nameless.

Around 1760, the nameless visionary whom we now call the Delaware Prophet lived in the Ohio Valley. He spoke to the Indians of different tribes and nations about the ills of alcohol. He also told them not to use their newly acquired guns to hunt. He said that these things would never be to the Indian what the hunting and war weapons of their fathers had always been. The Delaware

Prophet said that if his Indian people returned to their old ways, they would get their country back.

Years later, around 1810, another great prophet walked the Ohio Valley. His influence spread all the way from the Northeast to the Southeast. As far away as Florida and the mouth of the Mississippi River, the Indians were hearing of this prophet's visions and teachings.

Elskwatawa (the Open Door) was his name. He was Shawnee. Like the Delaware Prophet, he believed that alcohol was an evil among the People. He urged them to return to their old ways, to avoid contact with the white man whenever possible. He saw these things after he had collapsed from alcohol abuse himself and was thought to have died. Instead, he revived with stories of a dream that he had while he was apparently dead. He never touched alcohol again!

He and his brother Tecumtha nearly succeeded in establishing a united Indian nation with a true capital and spiritual center called Tippecanoe. It was located on the banks of the Wabash River in present-day Indiana. At no time in the history of the world had so many different tribes and nations unified! But the vision of Elskwatawa and the hopes of his brother Tecumtha died, for the prophet Elskwatawa did not follow the instructions of his brother. Warned by Tecumtha not to engage in battle, Elskwatawa nonetheless attempted to stop the superior forces of the United States army.

Elskwatawa was not a war leader, and his outnumbered warriors were defeated in a fierce battle by the army of General William Henry Harrison in 1811. General Harrison then torched the great town and Indian spiritual capital of Tippecanoe. It was a devastating blow to the new Indian nation, but it was an act that would one day help Harrison win the presidency of the United States with the popular slogan, "Tippecanoe and Tyler too." (Tyler was his running mate.)

Often, men of vision such as the prophets lack the power to rally great numbers of the People. But the Ottawa chief Pontiac was able to use the teachings and the spiritual strength of the Delaware Prophet to rally thousands of warriors to wage war against U.S. government soldiers in defense of his country. The great Shawnee leader Tecumtha used the teachings and spiritual power of his brother Elskwatawa to do likewise. Although Pontiac and Tecumtha had also foreseen the destruction that was to come, they were warriors!

Not only were the People hearing the visionaries and prophets of their time, but they were seeing the natural signs of things to come. There were omens everywhere, for even nature and the cosmic entities can be prophets of a kind. We need just observe and recognize the signs!

For example, in N. Scott Momaday's book about his Kiowa people, *The Way to Rainy Mountain*, he explains how the Kiowa, one evening in the autumn of 1832, were awakened by "brillant flashes of light."

They knew that these brilliant star-flashes were no ordinary meteor shower. White and silver balls streaked across the sky, falling from the heavens. Some were brighter than the morning star, and one is said to have been the size of the moon! This incident occurred just after the ancient Tai-ma bundle of the Kiowas had been stolen by the Osage. This sacred bundle helped the Kiowa on their journey after they emerged from the earth. It contained their power. Although it was returned later, the Kiowas had been heartbroken by the loss.

Then, a short time after the shooting stars were seen, the Kiowas entered into their first treaty with the United States. It was as if the falling stars were a sign, a cosmic prophecy, foretelling the destruction of the old ways. The flag of the United States bears stars. Today many Americans see the flag and the stars it bears as representing greatness. Many Native Americans, however, see the flag and the stars it bears as representing a country that has broken every treaty it ever signed with their people.

Signs from the sky were not all that the American Indians saw which made them realize that the end of the old ways was near. Like the Delaware Prophet and Elskwatawa, other men also saw this happening. They too saw it in their dreams and visions. They saw more than some of them could ever understand. And they anguished over not being able to change what they saw.

Perhaps the Indian prophets held old seeds nurtured by dreams of things to come. By planting the seeds in the minds of the People living, they reminded them of their responsibility to the future. From the prophets' dreams and visions, they were better able to encourage the People to hold on to the time-tested old ways. These ways meant living in harmony with each other and in balance with the natural world. These old ways meant knowing the past. Remember, ancient seeds can still take root and fulfill their promise of new life.

These special men of dreams and visions are also limited by their human experiences when interpreting what they see. These visions can become great burdens, and sometimes they are not what they appear to be. Other times these dreams and visions are the only hope for a desperate people.

A dozen years before the beginning of the twentieth century, out of the People's great despair would come a prophet of the Ghost Dance religion. He was a prophet of hope.

CHAPTER 5

Religion, Land, Life:

The Teachings and Visions of Wovoka and Black Elk

▲▲▲

O my children! O my children!
Here is another of your pipes — Héeyé!
Here is another of your pipes — Héeyé!
Look! thus I shouted — Héeyé!
Look! thus I shouted — Héeyé!
When I moved the earth — Héeyé!
When I moved the earth — Héeyé!

— Ghost Dance Song for the
New World to Cover the Old

▼▼▼

Two other very special examples of dreams and visions exist among the Native American holy men. They are the Paiute Indian called Wovoka and the Oglala Sioux Indian named Black Elk. Though of different tribes and separated by a thousand miles and one generation, Wovoka and Black Elk held two things in common. Not only did they receive great visions, but their visions were also prophecies. Each saw the Indian and Mother Earth emerging from the destruction wrought upon them. It was humanly impossible for them to interpret their visions fully, and neither lived to see his vision fulfilled.

Toward the end of the nineteenth century, the world, as the Indians saw it, was turning into their worst nightmare. The buffalo and many other native animals and birds were disappearing from North America. They were driven away from their homes as forests fell to farms and pastures replaced prairies. Fences and roads and train tracks cut the animals off from their Mother Earth. They were subdued and killed by the guns of people who took more than they needed.

As Big Elk had foreseen, a giant wave of civilization would crash upon this continent, often washing away any traces of what had once been here. Many of the people who rode upon the giant wave had little regard for the rights of things to live. They killed the native animals and birds, sometimes for food to supply their ever-increasing numbers, but most often, for profit or for pleasure.

The buffalo were shot and skinned for the value of their hides. The rest of the animal was wasted. Later, buffalo hunters and tourists shot thousands of buffalo from cross-country trains. They also killed elk and big-horn sheep. They took nothing but the life of the animals they killed, leaving them to rot in the sun. Oh, how the People cried! The elk and deer were killed so their heads or horns could serve as trophies. Sometimes the soldiers slaughtered them or encouraged their slaughter for money. The soldiers knew that animals like the buffalo provided food, clothing, tools, and shelter for the People, especially for those who lived on the Great Plains. The easiest way to kill Native Americans or to force them to surrender was to kill their food. Kit Carson may not have slaughtered animals to hurt the People, but he devastated the Navaho by burning their crops. Indians were in the way of "civilization." As the buffalo disappeared and the crops turned to ashes, the People starved.

Buffalo Bill received his name and his glory because he killed more buffalo than did any other man — he even boasted of such things. In his "Wild West Show," it is said that he had buffalo herded into a ring and bragged that he could kill one with every shot he fired. And before a paying audience, he tried!

The white man is not entirely to blame for such destruction; there were black buffalo soldiers who served in the U.S. army and raided Native American villages, Chinese laborers who helped to complete the Union Pacific Railroad and there were those among the People who were not without fault. Some of them also trapped and skinned animals for money. They shot birds for the money the fine feathers and precious plumes would

bring at the trading store. Sometimes they bought com-
modities with this money; other times it provided them
alcohol. Years earlier, they had been urged by the Delaware Prophet to keep the old ways of hunting and not to
use guns to kill animals. They had been warned by
Elskwatawa not to use alcohol. This is how the old ways
began to die.

Near the end of the nineteenth century, the animal and
bird nations were not the only endangered species. The
Native American population was seriously shrinking in
number as well. The Native People of North America
were on the verge of extinction, mainly because of new
and deadly diseases and broken treaties.

New sicknesses swept the People away like winds of
death, leaving whole tribes destroyed. Some diseases
were even spread deliberately by soldiers who know-
ingly took the blankets from their smallpox-ridden and
dying comrades and gave them to the People as gifts.

Many times the soldiers would unleash their newly
invented weapons of destruction on the Indians. Thunder-
ous batteries were capable of demolishing an entire Indian
village from miles away. The U.S. army also had automatic rifles and Gatling guns— the first machine guns.

This was the darkest of times for the People. The nineteenth century was ending. The United States was
growing and prospering, while American Indians were
clinging to survival. Their hearts were on the ground.
Their land was taken. The animals, their support, were
nearly gone. Their relatives had died by disease or war.
There was probably not an Indian family west of the

Mississippi who had not suffered the loss of loved ones. In desperation, more Indians turned to alcohol to momentarily relieve their suffering. From alcohol, more lives were lost.

The Native American people of the West had been driven to desperation. In his autobiography, *Land of the Spotted Eagle,* Chief Luther Standing Bear explains the confrontation between white and Native philosophies:

> We did not think of the great open plains, the beauitful rolling hills, the winding streams with tangled growth as "wild." Only to the white man was nature a "wilderness" and only to him was the land "infested" with "wild" animals and "savage" people. To us it was tame. Earth was bountiful and we were surrounded with the blessings of the Great Mystery.

The People needed hope. They needed to know that their country would not be ruined anymore. They needed this hope to carry on. One more time the People would struggle to make things beautiful again. And one more time they would dance in their circles and sing and hold their pipes high. And one more time they would unify as never before!

A dozen years before the beginning of the twentieth century, out of the People's despair came a prophet of hope. He was called Wovoka. The son of a dreamer named Tävibo. He was a Paiute Indian who never left the land of his birth in Mason Valley near Pyramid Lake, Nevada. When he was still a boy, his father died and he was adopted by a white family, made a Christian, and given the name Jack Wilson. He was to become a messiah to his Indian people, though he never claimed to be one.

At the age of thirty-five, Wovoka was given a great revelation during a total eclipse of the sun. He fell asleep and traveled to the ghost world. He described it as very beautiful. It was populated by all the Indians who had died before. Freed from the stress of life, they all seemed forever young and happy, engaged in doing the things that made them so.

According to James Mooney, an ethnologist (a person who studies and describes various cultures and folkways) who sought out and spoke with Wovoka, Wovoka said that during this revelation he was instructed to tell his people to be good and love one another. They must not fight. They must try to live peaceably with the white people. They shouldn't quarrel. They shouldn't steal. They must no longer engage in war. These teachings became the foundation of the Ghost Dance religion, and Wovoka was a prophet of that religion. It was a religion born of nonviolence.

If the People did these things, Wovoka said, they would be reunited with their friends and relatives in the ghost world. He was given a dance to help his people. As Wovoka's teachings spread, the Ghost Dance became a movement among many oppressed Native peoples, and it began to change. The dance was soon accompanied by songs for renewing the earth and for bringing back the animals and birds.

Desperate Indians began dancing the dances and singing the songs that would cause the world to open up and swallow all other people while the Indian and his friends would remain on this land, which would return to its beautiful and natural state. These events went beyond Wovoka's original instruction, but according to Mooney, they became a vital part of the Ghost Dance movement.

Wovoka instructed the People to continue dancing at intervals of five consecutive days. Other Indians from other nations began night dancing because that would allow them to hold their jobs and take care of their families during the day. If they continued to dance, they believed that they would not only "roll up the world," they would also be able to travel to that "other world" where they could visit with the ghosts of their dead relatives once again. And they did!

Indians from nearly all the tribes and nations west of the Mississippi sent selected travelers to Mason Valley. The messengers came. They listened and learned.

When they returned to their people, they instructed them on how to perform the Ghost Dance. It is important to remember that the Native Americans never sought to convert people to their religions. They had no missionaries. Wovoka taught only those who came to him.

This spiritual stirring among the Native Americans is now known as the Ghost Dance movement. The movement's influence spread from tribe to tribe like the promise of heavy clouds across the hills of dried and dying prairie grass. Because so many Indians were uniting as a result of Wovoka's teachings and the changes in his teachings provoked by desperation and hope, the new settlers became afraid.

As Chief Pontiac did with the teachings of the Delaware Prophet and as Tecumtha did with Elskwatawa's spiritual influence, some of the more militant factions of the Kiowas, Cheyennes, Arapahoes, and Sioux did with Wovoka's message. Inspired by the unity and promise of the Ghost Dance movement, they interpreted Wovoka's teachings to better fit their military needs. This interpretation was, once again, probably a result of desperation and the hope of regaining what was once theirs.

Instead of a religion of nonviolence, now these Indian warriors were dreaming designs to paint on their Ghost Dance shirts. Some of these dream paintings were medicine, and they would protect the Indians against soldiers' bullets. In one battle, a Kiowa warrior, wearing his Ghost Dance shirt with his dreamed symbols painted on it for protection, was wounded in his leg by a soldier's rifle. Rather than lose faith in his Ghost Dance medicine, the warrior returned home and made leggings for the next battle.

Faith is a strong medicine, and the symbols and spirits that came to the People in their Ghost Dance dreams were strong medicine. Then what went wrong?

Black Elk, a Native American holy man of the nineteenth and twentieth centuries, described the massacre of Ghost Dancers at Wounded Knee, South Dakota, in 1890. It was Christmas Eve when the soldiers surrounded the peaceful gathering of mostly old men, women, and children. He said that the soldiers demanded that the People turn in all their weapons. When this was done, a shot was fired and the soldiers let loose. Armed with automatic weapons and Gatling guns, the troops of the Seventh Cavalry simply slaughtered the people of the Ghost Dance.

Afterwards, more than a hundred Indian bodies were tossed into a mass grave and buried. Many of their Ghost Dance shirts were stolen by the soldiers for souvenirs. Some of the Indian People who tried to run away, including women and children, were shot and left to freeze in the snow.

Black Elk was a boy among the Lakota back then. He lived to be an old man, and all his life he tried desperately to fulfill the vision he received as a boy. In this vision, he too saw the devastation of what was to come:

> Again, and maybe for the last time on this earth, I recall the great vision you [Wakan-Tanka] sent me. It may be that some little root of the sacred tree still lives. Nourish it then, that it may leaf and bloom and fill with singing birds.

CHAPTER 6

Prophecies of Our Time

▲▲▲

The Emergence into the future Fifth World has begun. It is being made by humble people of little nations, tribes, and racial minorities.

— from the Hopi prophecy in Frank Waters's *Book of the Hopi*

▼▼▼

Prophecies are often filled with symbols that represent different things to different people. Often we have little way of knowing if some were truly spoken by the prophets who are said to have made them. Other prophecies are surrounded by an uncertainty, sort of like a fog that does not allow us to see clearly.

One of the most popular prophecies to emerge in the last twenty years is the prophecy of Deganawida. Again, how is one to know if indeed the Peacemaker himself made this prophecy? Perhaps we don't really know, but it is a prophecy that seems to prevail in this century.

According to this Iroquoian prophecy, three serpents and the American Indian will be involved. These serpents are white, black, and red. They may represent other races and nations. It was foreseen that the Indian would be nearly choked to death by the white serpent, who will take control over the Indian's country. Then, at some unknown point in time, a red serpent from the north will be momentarily accepted by the white serpent, but slowly the two would become involved in a great battle. It is said that the rivers will boil and the stench of death will be everywhere. The Indian, however, will be gathering on a hill and must not get involved in this fierce battle.

Then, the black serpent will become enraged at the white serpent and enter into the conflict against him. Meanwhile, the red serpent will be defeated and will leave the country of the Indian forever. Behind it will be a bloody trail. But the black serpent, taking advantage of the war-weary white serpent, will defeat him and look to the hill to conquer the Indian, who all this time has gathered his power. For some reason, the black serpent will choose not to engage the Indian in conflict and will leave, also never to bother him again.

At this point, a great light will appear coming from the east. The black serpent will flee in terror of it and the white serpent will head toward it, going east and away from the Indian.

This prophecy states that Deganawida will be that light, and he will return to his Indian people.

Other prophecies exist that have emerged in this century. The Hopi prophecies are probably the most well-known. Some of these prophecies have not been revealed to anyone but those elders who keep them. They remain in the protective custody of the respective Hopi elders and clans.

Much of what is known of the Hopi prophecies has come true. The description of cobwebs strung across the sky, for example, is symbolic of how the great power lines, drawing from the destruction of the land through the digging of coal and uranium, appear much like "cobwebs" strung across the sky.

According to Frank Waters's *Book of the Hopi*, a world war will start in the Middle East, and it will involve China as well. It will be a war in which religion is used in a great conflict over "material matters" such as the wealth that oil now provides. The prophecy predicts that the United States will be destroyed and that only those people of all races who are of good heart will emerge into the next world, the fifth. This world will begin when ancient seeds from plant forms of past worlds will emerge, be studied, and planted. Seeds are also being planted now in our hearts and in the sky as stars and mystical circles and symbols are forming in the wheat fields of England, the ice fields of Russia and the corn fields of North America. According to the Hopi and other native people, this "emergence" into the next world has already begun.

Again, there is much symbolism in prophecies, and the symbols can mean different things to different people.

Another prophecy came in the vision of a twentieth-century Native American holy man named Lame Deer. Before his death in the mid-1970s, Lame Deer's dreams and visions were recorded by Richard Erdoes in their classic book, *Lame Deer, Seeker of Visions.*

In one of his great visions, Lame Deer said that a "light man" or "light men" will appear on earth. They will have the capability to stop atomic power and electricity. Even Lame Deer shivered to think about the results of this. He said that too much electricity and atomic power is being used and that they make the world out of balance. When the lights go off, there will be riots and looting, rapes and chaos. People who have become too dependent on such power will be affected the most. This light man or men will also have the power to do good. Lame Deer believed that he or they would appear by the end of this century.

Not too bright a future to head into, is it, even if the light men come? As a matter of fact, according to these Native American prophecies, it's rather frightening. Whether or not we choose to believe them, one thing is certain: They do shake us up. Maybe that is what we need. These are the warnings. Humans must learn from the past. We must learn how to live more respectfully, in balance with this earth and sky and with each other, and we must do it soon. If we ignore the prophecies, this civilization would end, just like Chief Sealth said it would more than a century ago.

PART II

Dad's Signs, Now Mine

▼▼▼

CHAPTER 1

Words Are Arrows

▲▲▲

**Words are arrows
and can pierce you hard.**

**Anger drips
from the
wounds
of
words
used like
arrows.**

**And pain
is remembered
in the
scars.**

— White Deer of Autumn

▼▼▼

M r. Horn walked into the sixth-grade classroom. Without speaking, he picked up the chalk and wrote on the board, *Words are arrows*. Then he asked his students to say the first thing that came into their minds when he mentioned a particular race or nationality. Whatever they said, he'd write on the board.

Some of the students squirmed in their seats. Others glanced at each other with suspicious eyes. Perhaps Mr. Horn was kidding. Even the class thug, Wayne Cassidy, almost smiled — something he never did.

His comrade, Lincoln Crosswell, laughed. "We gonna get into trouble for what we say?" he asked.

Mr. Horn assured them that they wouldn't, but he did require them to be honest in their responses. He also asked them not to think too hard about it. For some students like Wayne and Lincoln, that wasn't a difficult request to follow. "Tell me about Italians," Mr. Horn said.

"What about Mazzada over there?" sneered Cassidy. "He gonna get mad or something?"

Mr. Horn glanced at David Mazzada. Bright, strong-looking, and of Italian descent, he was a special student. "He'll get his turn, Wayne. I assure you; everyone will get his turn." The students were spooked by the way Mr. Horn said that.

"What's this got to do with our lesson on American Indians?" asked Stephanie O'Neil. She was probably searching for a way not to do anything and to go to sleep, as she usually did.

"Maybe nothing, Stephanie. Maybe everything."

"Greasers!" bellowed Wayne. "Italians are greasers."

"Gangsters!" Stephanie shouted, surprising everyone because she was usually asleep by now. "You know, like that movie, 'The Mafia Father.' "

"I think you mean *The Godfather*, Steph," said Mr. Horn. "The Mafia is an organization of crime."

"Yeah," said another, "and they wear a lot of gold jewelry and stuff."

"That's because they're into gambling and smuggling," added Stephanie. "And aren't the men really hairy and the women all fat?"

Mr. Horn was writing their responses on the board as he had said he would. Occasionally he would wince as one of the word arrows struck, but the students couldn't see him. "What are Italians called?" he asked.

"Wops!" was the unanimous reply. Someone else said "Guinea." Cassidy emphasized "greaser" one more time.

David Mazzada sat in quiet disbelief. He wanted to defend his nationality, but too many students were yelling comments. Mr. Horn couldn't write them down fast enough. For the first time, David realized that he really didn't know much about being Italian.

He felt bad for his dad and mom. They worked hard. It hurt him to think that people thought of them this way. His dad had struggled to establish his own electrical business, and his mom was a nurse on the night shift at the local hospital.

Next, Mr. Horn wrote *black people* on the board. A wave of words washed over him.

"Niggers!" shouted some. "Buckwheat," laughed another. "They steal." "They do drugs!" exclaimed others.

"Good runners." "Yeah, good basketball players." "Not very smart at school, though."

"Rap music," yelled Laurie Barnes, eager to include herself in the "discussion." Laurie was considered by many boys and girls to be the school's most beautiful girl. Her long blond hair glistened. Her soft, rosy cheeks yielded to a wide, pretty smile. "Blacks are good dancers, but they swear a lot and do drugs and . . . they beat women!" The fact that she was sitting in front of Bernita didn't seem to matter. Maybe Laurie had never realized that Bernita was black.

Mr. Horn just kept writing. Bernita was one of his best students, particularly noted for her exceptionally well-written papers. She sat with almost the same expression as did David Mazzada. Lincoln Crosswell, who hadn't hesitated to reveal his ideas about Italians to the class, slouched silently at his desk.

"My father never beat no woman," he mumbled angrily.

"What about whites?" asked Mr. Horn. "Do you know anything about whites?"

Most of the students were white. Mr. Horn's question brought on a major silence in the room, but Lincoln Crosswell smashed it hard. His buddy in tyranny, Wayne Cassidy, sank into his desk as he braced for similar treatment. Wayne hadn't hesitated to express his ideas about blacks, and he had hurt Lincoln.

"Honkies!" cried Lincoln. "Rich honkies!"

"Poor athletes and pretty lazy," Bernita added softly.

"Yeah," said one white student. "Whites aren't good athletes, but they do much better in school."

"All white people care about is money!" snapped Lincoln. "And the reason you do good in school is because white people are always cheating."

"What about Asians and Orientals? We can't leave Yang out." Mr. Horn glanced at Yang and smiled. Yang was a creative boy born in the United States of a Thai father and Vietnamese mother. He grew up speaking three languages and hearing stories about how his parents had barely escaped the Vietnam War with their lives.

Mr. Horn's eyes scanned to Tai-Ling. She was Chinese and also a good student. Tai Ling's greatest gift was her art. All the kids admired her drawings.

"Slant eyes!" responded one student. "Chinks," added another. "Japs." "Gooks." The names poured out. "Yeah, they all know karate." "They speak funny."

"Germans?" asked Mr. Horn.

"Nazis!" shouted Wayne Cassidy, apparently recovered from Lincoln's idea of whites.

"Puerto Ricans?"

"Spics." "They never wash." "They do drugs and buy lots of jewelry."

"And the Irish — what do we know about them?"

"Shamrocks!" one student called out.

"They drink a lot." "They wear a lot of green."

These comments baffled Stephanie. She wasn't wearing green. Her parents drank only an occasional beer or wine. She had never seen them drunk.

"Don't they believe in leprechauns, Mr. Horn?" smiled Yang. "You know — those little people who live in the woods."

Mr. Horn wrote *leprechauns* on the board. "Let's switch to Jewish people," he continued.

"All they care about is money." "Yeah, they're really cheap."

"They wear those funny beanies and they've got big noses," added Stephanie — amazingly still awake!

"And what do people call Jews?" asked Mr. Horn, writing as fast as he could.

"Jew boy!" laughed one student.

"Kikes," added another.

"What about Jamil over there in the corner? His parents are Palestinian and Lebanese."

One student quickly exclaimed, "Terrorists!"

"Towel heads," snickered Lincoln. "They got all that money from oil, too."

"Yeah, and they got lots of wives," added Laurie. "You know, like herons or something like that."

Mr. Horn smiled and shook his head. "Herons are birds, Laurie. I think you mean *harems*.

"The French — what do we think about them?" asked Mr. Horn. This time he spotted Michael Roulet, who suddenly sat straight up. His face was very serious. He had been in the United States for only a year, but already was in advanced reading classes.

"Sexy women," said Cassidy. The whole class giggled when he said that.

"What do we call French people?"

Michael Roulet wouldn't give anyone else a chance to answer. "Oh, I know what they call me, Mr. Horn. They call me 'Frenchy' or 'french fry.' And I think it is stupid!"

Mr. Horn also included Mexicans, who most everyone agreed were called "wetbacks" and were "lazy" because they always took siestas. Everyone but Carlos Navales agreed.

Carlos thought about the meaning or the madness of what Mr. Horn was doing. Mr. Horn and his father were friends. Both taught at the same school. He knew they respected each other. That's what puzzled him. Carlos's dad wasn't lazy. He had two college degrees and spoke four languages fluently.

The students went on shouting words faster than the gush of water from a whale's blowhole. Steve Polawski got it really bad. It seemed everyone knew a "Polish joke."

Even pretty Laurie Barnes had to suffer, especially when the guys started shouting out how blondes were all "dumb"!

All Laurie could feel was hurt and anger.

The board was filled with descriptions of everyone's race or nationality. Everyone felt the pain of the "word arrows."

Mr. Horn turned, took a few steps back, and looked at the class. His students sat shamefully still, feeling foolish and embarrassed. The fun was over. Now they sat and stared at what they had said about each other. They stared at the piercing words.

Bernita spoke first. "Pretty bad, Mr. Horn. Isn't it?"

"Stereotypes are usually bad, Bernita. Worse, they are usually wrong. When we stereotype, we often take something negative about a few people and make it belong to a whole group or race of people." Mr. Horn walked to the back of the quiet room. He leaned against the bulletin board that displayed all their finest papers. For a few moments, he stared out the window. "If we're going to experience the pain of word arrows, I suggest that you make shields to defend yourselves," he said.

"Tomorrow we're going to learn some things about the American Indian. But first, I suggest that you start preparing your shields. I want you to write one paragraph responding to the stereotype of who you are. Then write one about a friend of yours in class responding to the stereotype of that person."

The bell rang suddenly. Everyone left, unusually quiet. Hands in his pockets, Mr. Horn walked slowly to the front of the room. He kept staring at the words he had scribbled on the board under the topic *Words are arrows*.

CHAPTER 2

Making Shields

▲▲▲

Shields were usually made of buffalo hides tightly stretched and finely decorated with dream or vision beings. If these dreams or visions included a bird of some kind, feathers from that bird were attached where the hide ended. The tightness and strength of the hide was vital protection to the warrior, but not more so than the design that was painted on it.

— White Deer of Autumn

▼▼▼

The next day everyone came prepared. Each student had completed the assignment — an amazing thing in itself. Before they could read their paragraphs aloud,

Mr. Horn gave them each a piece of cardboard. He opened a big book and showed them color pictures of what he called "American Indian shields."

Each shield was different. One had two moons and the stars of the Big Dipper painted on it. Another had the sun and blackbirds on it. One had turtles painted on it, and eagle feathers were hanging from it. One even had crows and creatures that looked like lizards painted on it, and crow feathers were tied almost all the way around. One had a rainbow stretched over a tree filled with all kinds of colorful birds.

Amazed and intrigued, the children studied the magical shields. Mr. Horn explained how important the shields were and how the Indians usually designed and made them from dreams and visions and signs of power.

"I want you to draw a shield on your piece of cardboard," Mr. Horn instructed. "It will serve as the cover for your paragraphs on stereotypes. When you're done, you can hang it in your room or elsewhere in your house. You can draw anything you want. But keep this in mind: Your shield's purpose is to protect you and to defend what you are."

The students began working immediately. They sketched and colored their Indian-style shields. When they had finished, Mr. Horn had them stand and show their shields to the class before they read their papers. Some even tied string to their shields to hold them.

"They look almost real," said Lincoln while he examined his shield closely.

"They're as real as you believe they are," answered Mr. Horn.

David Mazzada went first. He held up a shield of crossed baseball bats with four footballs stationed North and South and East and West. David told about the Italian artists Michelangelo and Leonardo da Vinci. He told about the Hall of Fame baseball player Joe DiMaggio and the great quarterback Dan Marino.

Laurie told about the famous television journalist Barbara Walters. Certain world leaders and renowned people would interview only with her — no one else. "Not too shabby for a blonde," she said.

Next, Yang spoke of Vietnamese and Thai culture. He shared his knowledge of Buddhism and reincarnation and his lack of knowledge of karate. Yang drew a fire-breathing dragon on his shield.

Tai-Ling read about the great Chinese philosopher and teacher named Confucius. She also discussed Chinese culture and completed her paper by reading a beautiful Chinese poem. Tai-Ling drew two cranes on her shield. They seemed ready to fly at any moment.

Bernita read poems by Nikki Giovanni, a famous black woman poet, and a passage from Alice Walker, a Pulitzer Prize–winning writer. She also read a piece about how trees have feelings and how we should respect them. A big flowering tree colored her shield.

Wayne Cassidy said that he had found out that if it weren't for black people like Martin Luther King, he and Lincoln never would have become friends. He admitted that he hated riding the school bus for an hour, but he said that it was worth it just to see Lincoln.

Wayne put a Phantom F-4 complete with heat-seeking missiles and rockets on his shield. A fierce eagle stretched out his wings in the background. Paper feathers hung from it just like the real ones in the pictures that Mr. Horn had shown.

Of course, Lincoln said that he trusted Wayne more than anyone else. He admitted that in all the years he'd known Wayne and as many times as he'd seen Wayne fail a test, he'd never seen Wayne cheat. As for money, Wayne was usually just as broke as he was. A tiger decorated Lincoln's shield.

Stephanie O'Neil read her paper on great Irish writers. She chose as her shield a green shamrock under a rainbow. In the rainbow was a poem by William Butler Yeats.

As for Jamil, he wrote about his people's need for their own nation. His shield displayed the Palestinian flag.

All in all, it was quite a day. No one was happier than Steve Polawski. He had discovered that one of the world's greatest astronomers was a Polish man named Copernicus. Steve designed a beautiful shield of stars.

The students all felt differently than they had the day before. They learned from Judy Burnette that a *yarmulke* is not a "beanie." A *yarmulke* is worn for religious reasons. They also learned that being stingy is not a trait to give to a whole people, especially when Judy, a pretty Jewish girl without a "big nose," had given thirty-five cents to Wayne Cassidy that day for lunch.

Yesterday, some of Mr. Horn's students left angry. A few left ashamed. The others were either embarrassed or hurt. Mr. Horn told them that words can be arrows and can pierce even the strongest of hearts.

Today was different. Their knowledge of their heritages helped make them proud. The knowledge of who their friends were made them better friends. Their shields were the symbols and protectors of their knowledge. They were beautiful shields, powerful shields.

One of the students asked Mr. Horn why he thought that people made up such awful names and things about each other.

"If you're ashamed of yourself or your roots, then you feel superior to other people when you degrade them or make fun of them. It's easier to degrade people who are different. Does that make sense?"

They nodded, although he suspected that they didn't yet understand.

"It's easier to hate, even kill, someone who is less than human. Such horrible names, like the ones we heard here yesterday, belittle people, degrade them, make them into something less than human to the one who speaks the names.

"Unfortunately, these names are piercing arrows that strike at the very heart of a person. No matter how strong you think you are, sometimes the arrows of ignorance and hate hurt you badly. You yourself want to cry or to scream back hate. That's why you now have your shields. They'll protect you.

"Now we are ready for our lesson.

"I'd like you to write a paragraph explaining what you know about American Indians. Make it just like your first assignment. Don't look anything up. Write down just what you have learned from school, parents, television, movies, or whatever.

"Also, I want you to use any words that you associate with Indians. Don't think too hard." Mr. Horn laughed. "That goes for you too, Cassidy." Everybody laughed, including Wayne Cassidy.

CHAPTER 3

← →

All I Know
About Indians

▲▲▲

**"The only good Indians I ever saw,
were dead."**

— General Sheridan

▼▼▼

It had rained throughout the night, and it was still rain-
ing. Everyone in the school felt sullen. Although the
classroom lights were on, the room still seemed dark.

Mr. Horn was proud of his students. He hung their
papers around the room, between pictures of black, white,
Asian, and American Indian people already on the walls.

Again, he walked into the room and wrote *Words are
arrows* on the board. Underneath he added *All I know*

about Indians. The students shuffled their assignments, waiting. "Fire!" he commanded.

"Squaw!" called out one student. "One arrow," Mr. Horn thought as he wrote.

"Redskins!" said another.

"Scalping!"

"Rain dances."

Mr. Horn glanced up and scanned the room. He looked out the window at the rain falling heavily. Then he looked back at the students. He winked. Some of the kids smiled.

"Corn," declared one student.

"Good," responded Mr. Horn. "Keep going."

"They got red skin," Wayne Cassidy said, as if it were fact.

"No they don't!" interrupted Laurie. "They've got sort of a copper-colored skin, like a tan. And their hair is jet black."

"And real straight and long," added Lincoln, not to be outdone by Wayne. "They're real fierce warriors, and they paint their faces. They yelp and hoot a lot around a fire. War dancing, I believe it's called."

Wayne laughed, "Maybe it's because they're always smoking peace pipes." He wouldn't let Lincoln get one up on him. Wayne had seen Indians smoking peace pipes in the movies. He wanted to know if they smoked "dope" in them.

Mr. Horn just blinked his eyes. It seemed everybody was wondering the same thing. "You know what I mean, Mr. Horn — marijuana," Wayne whispered. "Don't they smoke . . . it . . . or some other weird stuff in their pipes?"

Mr. Horn sighed. "I'll put it on the board, Wayne. Anything else, kids?" he asked.

Jamil raised his hand. "I don't believe the Indians have cause to shave."

Everyone laughed. They all agreed that Indians don't have beards.

"Where did Indians come from?" Mr. Horn asked.

Stephanie, still awake, said that Indians came from Asia. "Weren't they mongrels, or something like that?"

"I think you mean Mongols, from the Mongolian people," Mr. Horn explained.

Tai-Ling said that Indians lived in tepees and wandered around the country picking berries and hunting.

Wayne agreed. Indians ate raw meat and fish. They spoke a funny kind of English.

"How!" laughed Lincoln. "Me listening."

"Yeah, like that, Mr. Horn."

"Don't they have lots of gods?" asked Judy Burnette.

"And don't they live on reservations that the government gave them?" asked Bernita. "I'm not sure, but I think they have to have special permission to leave."

"I know they like nature," added Michael Roulet. "We studied something about them in France."

"Okay," said Mr. Horn. "That should do it for now. Besides, my arm is getting tired, and the bell is about to ring. I want you to go to the library in the next day or two and find a book about American Indians. Better yet, try to find a book written by an American Indian."

The bell rang, and everyone, as usual, raced out. They were careful to protect their shields. Mr. Horn walked to the door. He was about to switch off the light and leave when another teacher stepped in.

"Hey, I heard what you were doing in here," he said. He stared at the words on the board, then shook his head. "Sign of the times, Horn. Sign of the times."

Before closing the door, Mr. Horn gazed back into the classroom. "I guess so," he muttered.

Then he closed it. Locked inside were some of the most important reasons why an Indian, like his dad, had to suffer from misunderstanding and humiliation all his life. Although he locked those reasons in for the night, Mr. Horn knew they'd be there to face him first thing in the morning.

Next time he would bring his shield!

CHAPTER 4

Mr. Horn's Shield

▲▲▲

**If a man loses anything and goes back
and looks carefully for it, he will find it. ...
I feel that my country has gotten a bad
name, and I want it to have a good one; it
used to have a good one; and I sit sometimes and wonder who has given it a bad
name.**

— Sitting Bull

▼▼▼

That night the rain stopped. The earth had drunk
fully, and the crickets sang their appreciation. The
great elms and oaks were nourished, as were the grasses
and other plants.

Mr. Horn put down the book he was reading. He
stared at the shield hanging over the fireplace. It spoke

to him. It talked to his mind without words or sound and told him it needed to be taken down.

He stood before it, hesitating. This shield had hung in the living room, protecting his home for twenty-five years. The signs painted on the shield were his dad's. Now they were his too. The world and the way people think had changed very little.

The diameter of the shield was twenty inches. The symbol of the Four Directions prominently covered the entire circle of the shield, dividing it into four equal parts, each a different color.

His father had made the shield for him. First he had taken a willow branch and bent it into a circle. Then he had stretched deerskin around it, tying the deerskin to the branch.

Mr. Horn remembered how his father had handed him the unpainted shield. "I want you to paint it," he began. "Start with the East. It represents our birth. At birth we begin the Circle of Life. We paint the East yellow to stand for the sun. It is the symbol for birth and rebirth. Knowledge and truth are its Powers of Life."

His dad explained how warm winds come from the South. Mr. Horn remembered painting a symbol for the South in red at the bottom of the shield. Red represents the warmth of life, the blood of life that all creatures share. The South stands for life in its prime, like the vitality and heat of summer.

To the left, opposite the yellow East, is the West. Mr. Horn recalled painting this part black. His dad explained that it is the sign of mystery. It represents the night. He said that black could also be the sign of ignorance and hate. If man, in the autumn of his years, doesn't seek the wisdom in the Mystery of Life, he will remain ignorant. He will always be in the dark, afraid and sometimes dangerous.

At the top of the shield, opposite the South, is the North. He painted it white. His dad explained how white is the sign for purity in the way we look at the world, in our lives, and in how we think and how we speak. Mother Earth is mostly covered with cleansing snow in this wintry time of the yearly cycle. "It is the great white blanket that purifies her and keeps her strong."

Then his dad said, "Someday, your hair will turn white like the snow. This is the sign of a man who has lived a full life. At least, that's what it should mean. White hair means wisdom acquired through living experiences. It is also the time to prepare for the Great Change."

The Great Change, he explained, is that time when the spirit leaves our body and we die. Actually, we don't really die. Our body simply returns to Mother Earth and our spirit to the Great Mystery and Giver of Life. We will live on in the memory of the living and in the love we leave behind. "These things," his father said, "are what your loved ones will need to continue when you are gone."

Mr. Horn hung eagle and owl feathers from the sides of the shield. His dad said that they came from special birds. The eagle feather is the sign of a person's bravery in seeking wisdom. You can earn one defending your people, defending what you know to be right. The eagle feather is also the award for a person's contribution to the People and the world.

The owl feathers have special meaning too. Owl has the power to see in the darkness of night. Owl can also see through the darkness that comes from ignorance, fear, or hate.

"If you are to live in this world today, you need to wear these feathers on your shield. They have helped me through many a dark time in my life," his dad said.

Lastly, his dad explained that each color on the shield represents a race of people. Each race is equal in the Circle of Life shield. "Appreciate the gifts and beauty of all cultures and races," he said.

This was the shield that Mr. Horn would bring to school the next day. Behind it he would carry books. In these books was recorded the wisdom of the People.

CHAPTER 5

Arrows of Truth

▲▲▲

**Oh, my country 'tis of thy sermons,
  orations
That deny us God's grace shed on thee
Can't you see, can't you see, oh say can't
  you see
What you've done to my people, my
  land, and to me?**

> — from "A Chant to Lure Honor,"
>
> by White Deer of Autumn

▼▼▼

Everyone crowded around Mr. Horn's desk to see his Four Directions shield. Even kids from other classes stopped by to see it. And, as his dad had done with him, Mr. Horn took the time to explain at least some of its many meanings and symbols.

A few of his students had gone to the library and found books on Indians. David Mazzada explained that he didn't have time to go yet, but he brought in his Cleveland Indians baseball cards to show. And Lincoln Crosswell explained that he didn't get to the library either. He brought his Washington Redskins football card of Doug Williams, the black quarterback. Lincoln stated proudly that Doug Williams had won the Superbowl for the Redskins that year.

Mr. Horn studied the cards and asked if he could keep them for a while. "Sure," they said. Then class began.

Mr. Horn started with the word *squaw,* since that was the first "word arrow" shot at the board. He asked what this word meant. Just about everyone said that a squaw is an Indian woman.

He picked up one of the books and began to read. "'The word *squaw* probably comes from the Iroquois word *otsiskwa*. The French shortened it to squaw. It means female sex part.'" Then he closed the book.

A silence filled the room.

"Why would they call an Indian woman that, Mr. Horn?"

"Because that's how some European men viewed Indian women then — maybe all women. If you can think of the English word for the 'female sex part,' then that's what it's like for an Indian woman to be called a 'squaw.'"

The next word was *redskin*. Mr. Horn read a story about how some white people hated Indians because Indians had the land. The white people wanted the land, but the Indians didn't want to leave. The white people kept calling them "redskins" to show that they felt Indians were inferior to them.

Mr. Horn held up the football card and asked what race they thought Doug Williams is. Everyone, of course, responded "black." Lincoln didn't, though. He just listened.

"I wonder how he'd feel," said Stephanie, "if they called his team the Washington Blackskins?"

"Why do they do that, Mr. Horn?" asked Bernita. "That would be like calling a team the Washington Niggers or Washington Honkies. I was reading last night that Indians don't have red skin at all. Their skin can be just about any color. And besides, the book said that a lot of Indians prefer to be called by their tribal names. Some Indians wish to be called Native Americans."

"Very good, Bernita," Mr. Horn replied. "The team owner says the word *redskin* honors the Indian. If American Indian leaders, including the president of the National Congress of American Indians, feel that this word is insulting, then the owner is wrong."

Mr. Horn held out his hand. "I want you to look at the color of my hand." Everybody did. "This is the hand of a Native American. It is not red, or even tan. Although I have other racial blood mixed in my veins too, I am a Native American because of my heart."

His eyes seemed suddenly watery. His lips pressed together tightly, as if he were holding back a flood of feelings. "I never told you, because I didn't want anyone to know. I guess I just couldn't bear any more pain from society's arrows."

This didn't come as much of a shock to the class. Some said that they suspected he was Indian all along.

"That's cool, Mr. Horn," his students said. "We respect you."

Mr. Horn smiled. He explained that scalping was introduced to this hemisphere by some of the Dutch, French and English. "It was these European people who cut off the heads of Native Americans and brought them in for money, a bounty. Man, woman, child — it didn't matter. Only the money."

He said that when the heads of the Indian people became too cumbersome to carry, the Europeans began taking scalps to prove they had killed Indians. "Indians later imitated the practice, but not for money. More importantly, they didn't take the scalps of women and children."

He held up David Mazzada's Cleveland Indians baseball card. On it was a strange and funny-looking comic-strip character. The Indian face was red, with a huge nose and big teeth. David said it was called "Chief Wahoo." It was the team's symbol.

"How would you feel if this were done to you?" Mr. Horn asked. "How do you think I feel when I see my people displayed in such a disrespectful and humiliating way? For twenty years Native Americans have tried to get the city of Cleveland and the team's owners to change that wretched thing. My dad was Indian, children. He didn't look like that, and neither did my mother or my grandparents. I don't look like that.

Mr. Horn explained, "Indians don't all look alike. They don't all look like the Hollywood stereotype of the

Plains Indians. Even Crazy Horse didn't have long, straight black hair and a full-time tan. He had curly brown hair and fair skin. And Indians today vary in skin, hair, and eye color as much as anyone. They don't walk around with signs on their backs saying, 'I am an Indian.'

"One of the most well-known Indian actors in Hollywood was Iron Eyes Cody. Cody used to describe how the movie directors spray-painted Indians 'copper' before a film so they would look 'authentic.' "

Mr. Horn also said that one film producer, wanting to hire "real Indians," wound up casting Puerto Ricans and Cubans in his film because the Indians who came for the parts weren't dark enough.

He went on to say that some Indians today have long hair. Others have short hairstyles. They may dance any dance, although some still carry on their traditional dances as well. "Don't make fun of the Indian's power to bring rain or sunshine through song and dance. Beliefs are what enabled them to do this," he said. "These beliefs have kept them alive for tens of thousands of years."

Then he showed some old photographs of Indians. Some of the men had mustaches. One Cherokee chief, Tah-chee, was drawn with a heavy beard. Tah-chee did, in fact, have a beard, but no one ever mistook him for a white man. Tah-chee was one of the Cherokee chiefs who never surrendered or signed a treaty.

Mr. Horn emphasized that neither the United States government nor the Canadian government ever "gave" Native Americans reservation land. "This land has always been Indian land," he said.

As Mr. Horn read from the books, he held his Four Directions shield.

Mr. Horn talked about the importance of the pipe; to Indians, it is sacred. When an Indian smokes his pipe, he is praying to the Great Mystery, which we might think of as God. To an Indian, the pipe is as sacred as the Bible or the Koran.

Only tobacco and special herbs, such as *kinickinick* from the bark of the red willow, were placed in its bowl. Smoking was not to get you "high," but to help you connect your mind and heart with all things. He explained that it is called the "peace pipe" because Native Americans often have bound their words of peace through a formal smoking of the pipe.

"A peace or treaty made with the pipe was simply unbreakable in the minds of Native Americans. Unfortunately, the United States government did not share that belief. I can't think of a single treaty with my people that the U.S. government has honored — and we signed about 400 treaties."

When the bell rang, the kids gathered around Mr. Horn's desk. Some touched the Four Directions shield; others looked over the books. David and Lincoln said that Mr. Horn could keep the cards if he wanted. Maybe he could use them for other kids as he did today.

Mr. Horn smiled and said, "Thanks." When everyone had left, he picked up his books and his shield and shut the door. Standing in the hallway, he felt very tired. He felt old. He leaned against the door to rest. A numbness reached from his left shoulder to his hand. A sharp pain encircled his chest like a tightening steel wire. He took several short breaths.

Suddenly, two unfamiliar students raced up, laughed, and shouted "How!" with their palms raised. But when they saw the shield, their smiles and taunting laughter vanished. They fled like blue jays chased by an owl.

"Sign of the times, Horn," said that teacher again, passing by and shaking his head. "Sign of the times."

Mr. Horn nodded and glanced down at the shield. He clutched it tightly. "Dad's signs, now mine," he whispered to himself. "Dad's signs, now mine."

ABOUT THE AUTHOR

Noted author and lecturer Gabriel Horn was given the name "White Deer of Autumn" by his uncles, Meta–comet and Nippawanock, and by Princess Red Wing of the Narragansett tribe, Wampanoag nation. He has taught in reservation schools, American Indian Movement (AIM) survival schools, public schools, and junior colleges. He helped develop the curriculum and was head teacher at the Red School House in St. Paul, Minnesota. He was cultural arts director of the Minneapolis American Indian Center from 1980 to 1982 and helped establish the Minneapolis American Indian Art Gallery and the Living Traditions Museum. For his work in Indian rights, he was nominated for the Human Rights Award in the state of Minnesota.

Gabriel Horn has a master's degree in English and currently devotes his time to lecturing, teaching, and writing. He is a teacher in Florida as well as a member of the National Committee on American Indian History and an advisor to the Native American national newspaper, *Indigenous Thought*. He lives on the Florida coast with his wife, Simone, an Ojibway, close to Mother Earth and the natural world that is so precious to him.

ABOUT THE ILLUSTRATOR

Shonto Begay is a Native American artist who specializes in multicultural illustrations. His other works include *The Mud Pony,* a Native American story, and *Lluvia,* a Hispanic children's book. He lives in Kayenta, Arizona, with his family. His illustrations for *Native People, Native Ways* accurately detail the traditional dress, architecture, and art of the many different Native tribes in the various regions of the Americas throughout history.

ACKNOWLEDGMENTS

The "Native People, Native Ways" series would not have been accomplished without the support and assistance of my wife, Simone, and the sacrifices made by my loving children: Ihasha, Calusa, and Carises. Without Jay Johnson's belief in my work and Paige Graham's ability to work with draft after draft of each manuscript, and without Paige's constant reminders for me to listen to the ghost voices, these books would not reflect the quality that they have. I'm also grateful to the publishers of Beyond Words, Cynthia Black and Richard Cohn, who recognized the quality of the series and the needs that the books can help fulfill. Their proofreader, Marvin Moore, and Native American curriculum specialist, Chris Landon, fine-tuned the books in such a way as to make us all proud. And to Fred Brady and the other elders who sent their prayers into the Mystery that these books would become a reality for our children and grandchildren, I give my deepest gratitude. I would also like to thank my friend and agent, Sandra Martin, who continues to encourage me to write. I'm grateful to Shonto Begay for his spark of creativity that will help children to see Native people in a Native way. And lastly, I wish to acknowledge all the elders who took the time to teach me, and all the writers whose spirit enabled them to share what they too have learned from the Native People and Native Ways of this land.

Other Native American Children's Books
from Beyond Words Publishing, Inc.

THE NATIVE AMERICAN BOOK OF KNOWLEDGE

Author: White Deer of Autumn
Illustrator: Shonto Begay
96 pages, $4.95 softbound, ages 10-12

Investigates the fascinating and controversial origins of the People, based on tales from various tribes, scientific evidence, and archaeological finds. Discusses several key figures in the Americas, including Deganawida, Hyonwatha, and others who have had a mystical and spiritual impact on the Native people.

THE NATIVE AMERICAN BOOK OF LIFE

Author: White Deer of Autumn
Illustrator: Shonto Begay
96 pages, $4.95 softbound, ages 10-12

Speaks of the great importance of children in the Native way of life; about their pastimes, how they are named, initiated into everyday society, taught, disciplined, and cared for. A fictional, magical story about children visiting a Native museum and learning about the many practices relating to food and the People: food growing and gathering practices, feasting traditions, and food contributions.

THE NATIVE AMERICAN BOOK OF WISDOM

Author: White Deer of Autumn
Illustrator: Shonto Begay
96 pages, $4.95 softbound, ages 10-12

Explores the fascinating belief system of the People, from the concept of the Great Mystery, or Wakan-Tanka, to the belief that all life is sacred and interrelated. A tribal medicine man visits a contemporary classroom and the children are amazed at what he has to tell them about the traditions and power of his people.

CEREMONY IN THE CIRCLE OF LIFE

Author: White Deer of Autumn
Illustrator: Daniel San Souci
32 pages, $6.95 softbound, ages 6-10

The story of nine-year-old "Little Turtle," a young Native American boy growing up in city without the knowledge of his ancestors' beliefs. He is visited by "Star Spirit," who introduces him to his heritage and his relationship to all things in the "Circle of Life." Little Turtle also learns about nature and how he can help to heal the Earth.

THE GREAT CHANGE

Author: White Deer of Autumn
Illustrator: Carol Grigg
32 pages, $14.95 hardbound, ages 3-10

A Native American tale in which a wise grandmother explains the meaning of death, or the Great Change, to her questioning granddaughter. This is a story of passing on tradition, culture, and wisdom to the next generation. It is a moving tale for everyone who wonders about what lies beyond this life. Watercolor illustrations by internationally acclaimed painter Carol Grigg.

COYOTE STORIES FOR CHILDREN: TALES FROM NATIVE AMERICA

Author: Susan Strauss
Illustrator: Gary Lund
50 pages, $10.95 hardbound, $6.95 softbound, ages 6-12

Storyteller Susan Strauss has interspersed Native American coyote tales with true-life anecdotes about coyotes and Native wisdom. These stories illustrate the creative and foolish nature of this popular trickster and show the wisdom in Native American humor. Whimsical illustrations throughout.

SUGGESTED READINGS

PERMISSIONS:

Acknowledgment is gratefully made to the following authors and publishers who have granted permission to use selected quotations from their publications:

Carter, Forrest. *The Education of Little Tree.* Albuquerque, New Mexico: University of New Mexico Press, 1986.

Neihardt, John G. *Black Elk Speaks.* Lincoln, Nebraska: University of Nebraska Press, 1979.

Standing Bear, Luther. *Land of the Spotted Eagle.* Lincoln, Nebraska: University of Nebraska Press, 1969.

Track, Soge. "Indian Love Letter." *South Dakota Review* vol. 1, no. 2 (1969): p. 136.

NOTES ON SOURCES:

Momaday, N. Scott. *Way to Rainy Mountain.* New York: Ballintine Books, 1976.

The Council on Interracial Books for Children. *Chronicles of American Indian Protest.* Greenwich, Connecticut: Fawcett Publications, 1971.

Brown, Dee. *Bury My Heart at Wounded Knee.* New York: Holt, Rinehart & Winston, Inc., 1970.

Goldman, Jeffrey, Ph.D. *American Genesis.* New York: Summit Books, 1981.